IN-LINE SKATING

SPORTS CHALLENGE

DAVID ARMENTROUT

The Rourke Book Co., Inc.
Vero Beach, Florida 32964

David Armentrout specializes in nonfiction writing and has had several book series published for primary schools. He resides in Cincinnati with his wife and two children.

PHOTO CREDITS:
© Armentrout: page 15; © Kim Karpeles: page 18, 19; © Jed Jacobsohn/Allsport: Cover; © Al Bello/Allsport: pages 4, 12, 13; © Chris Covatta/Allsport: page 6; © Mike Powell/Allsport: page 10; © Nathan Bilow/Allsport: pages 16, 21, 22; © Chuck Mason/Intl Stock: pages 7, 9

EDITORIAL SERVICES:
Penworthy Learning Systems

Library of Congress Cataloging-in-Publication Data

Armentrout, David, 1962 -
   In-line skating / by David Armentrout.
      p. cm. — (Sports challenge)
   Includes index.
   Summary: Presents basic information on the essential skills, techniques, and equipment for in-line skating.
   ISBN 1-55916-222-8
   1. In-line skating—Juvenile literature. [1. In-line skating.]
I. Title II. Series: Armentrout, David, 1962 -   Sports challenge.
GV859.73.A76 1997
796.21—dc21   97–13006
                                                            CIP
                                                            AC

Printed in the USA

TABLE OF CONTENTS

In-Line Skating

In-line skating (IN lyn SKAYT ing) is one of the fastest growing sports in the world. Few sports have become as popular in such a short time.

Also called rollerblading, or just blading, in-line skating is enjoyed by people of all ages. With the proper equipment and a little practice, you can join the millions of people who are in-line skaters—if you're not already one of them.

Whether you are interested in speed skating, roller hockey, extreme skating, or just cruising, in-line skating offers something for everyone.

In-line skating is great exercise.

THE IN-LINE SKATE

In-line skating was invented by two brothers from Minnesota. Avid ice hockey players, the Olson brothers were looking for a way to practice their sport in the summer.

In-line racers use skates with five wheels.

Roller hockey is a popular neighborhood game.

The Olson brothers decided to replace the blades on their ice hockey skates with a row of plastic wheels. The new in-line skates were an instant success.

In time the Olson brothers started a company called Rollerblade, Inc. It was the first of many companies to make in-line skates.

BUYING THE RIGHT PAIR OF SKATES

Don't be fooled by inexpensive skates. They wear easily and may end up costing you more money in the long run.

It is important to buy good quality skates. Shop for name brands. Small skates, or junior sizes, may have three wheels while the larger sized skates will have four.

Buy skates that have a snug fit—but not too tight. If you purchase skates that don't fit properly, they may end up in the back of a closet.

A proper skate gives your foot support when skating.

SAFETY GEAR

Once you have invested in a good pair of in-line skates, don't skimp on the safety gear. In-line skating is an action sport. Serious injury may occur if you don't wear safety equipment.

A good quality helmet is needed to protect your head. **Wrist guards** (RIST GAHRDZ) are worn to prevent serious hand and wrist injuries.

Don't forget the knee and elbow pads! They are worth their weight in gold if you should happen to fall. Even experts fall, but their safety gear is always in place.

Wearing all the safety gear can help prevent injuries.

LET'S GET ROLLING

Choose a smooth level surface away from traffic to learn your new sport. Begin by putting on all the safety equipment.

In-line skating equipment comes in many styles and colors.

In-line skating is a fun sport that can be shared with friends.

Now get rolling! Keep your knees bent and your weight centered over your skates. Gently push off with one skate, keeping the other skate pointed forward. You're skating! Now try pushing off with the opposite foot.

After some practice you will be trying **crossovers** (KRAWS O verz), backward skating, and **sidesurfing** (SYD SERF ing).

STOPPING METHODS

In-line skates are equipped with a heel brake that is mounted on the rear of one or both skates. As you glide, slide your brake skate forward while lifting the toe. The brake will touch the pavement, slowing you down.

Another stopping method is the **T-stop** (T stahp). As you glide, lift one skate and turn it sideways, dragging it behind the other skate. The position of the skates forms a T. As you become more skilled you will learn other methods of stopping.

Some in-line skates have heel brakes mounted on both skates.

SPEED SKATING AND EXTREME SKATING

Speed skaters race against each other at very high speeds. These expert skaters reach speeds of 25 miles an hour and more! They compete in races varying from one-third mile (500 meters) to 62 miles (100 kilometers).

Extreme skaters practice their sport on a special ramp called a **half pipe** (HAF pyp). These highly skilled skaters skate down one side of the ramp and up the other side often "getting air" at the top. Only expert skaters should attempt the half pipe.

Sidesurfing is done on a smooth curved wall.

ROLLER HOCKEY

One of the most popular forms of in-line skating is roller hockey. Roller hockey teams play all over the world, and some teams compete in the summer Olympics.

Young roller hockey players wear protective shin guards and face masks.

The National Hockey League sponsors roller hockey competitions.

Roller hockey is only slightly different from ice hockey. Roller hockey teams have five players; ice hockey teams have six. **Checking** (CHEK ing) and other forms of body contact are not allowed in roller hockey but are commonly seen in ice hockey.

The protective gear and clothing are much the same in both sports, except roller hockey players use special in-line skates rather than ice skates.

CARING FOR IN-LINE SKATES

The wheels and **bearings** (BAIR ings) on in-line skates need regular maintenance. The owner's manual tells how to remove and rotate the wheels and clean the bearings.

Three things determine how fast the wheels wear: the surface skated on, the weight of the skater, and how often the skates are used. Keep the wheels clean and replace them when they look worn.

Cleaning the dirt and mud from the outside of the skates and caring for all the moving parts will help keep your skates rolling smoothly.

Cleaning and caring for your in-line skates will help them last longer.

GLOSSARY

bearings (BAIR ings) — steel balls that allow wheels to turn smoothly

checking (CHEK ing) — physical contact that slows or stops an ice hockey player in action

crossovers (KRAWS O verz) — repeatedly crossing one skate in front of the other

half pipe (HAF pyp) — a ramp shaped like a half-circle used by in-line skaters to perform trick maneuvers

in-line skating (IN lyn SKAYT ing) — skating in boots with a single row of wheels attached to their soles

sidesurfing (SYD SERF ing) — gliding in a circle by setting the heels of the in-line skates to face each other (see page 16)

T-stop (T stahp) — a stopping method for in-line skaters in which one skate is dragged behind the other, forming a T

wrist guards (RIST GAHRDZ) — safety gear made with soft foam and hard plastic to protect wrists and hands against serious injuries

A young skater performs for a crowd.

INDEX